How to Set Up a Token Economy

Teodoro Ayllon, Ph.D.
Sandra M. McKittrick, Ph.D.

8700 Shoal Creek Boulevard
Austin, Texas 78758

BF
637
.B4
A9
1982
148164
Feb. 1990

Printed in the United States of America
ISBN 0-89079-069-8

Additional copies of this book (#1015)
may be ordered from

·8700 Shoal Creek Boulevard
Austin, Texas 78758

Contents

Foreword

How to set up a Token Economy makes a major contribution to the goal of the series which is to make behavioral procedures available to parents, teachers, nurses, attendants, aides and other professionals and paraprofessionals who are responsible for managing and teaching appropriate behavior. It is fitting that Teodoro Ayllon, who with Nathan Azrin (one of the editors of this series) pioneered the use of systematic token economies in institutions, is its author. Their earlier book, **The Token Economy,** remains a classic, the definitive work on the topic.

This manual describes the use of token economies in a distilled form so that practitioners in homes, classrooms, institutions and communities can quickly grasp the essential elements of a token system and set one up to meet their needs in their own environments.

The impact that token systems have as a teaching tool for bringing improvement of behavior in a positive way remains one of the major contributions of behavioral psychology. This is especially true in situations where less-structured systems have been ineffective. An important dimension of a well-managed token economy that is sometimes overlooked is that it not only provides a structure for the person whose behavior it is designed to change, but the system also provides a structure that brings about a profound change in the behavior of the person who manages the token system. It does so in the following ways:

1. It causes the manager to clearly specify for himself and for the client which behaviors are important to change.
2. It increases the probability that the manager will provide positive consequences for clients who exhibit appropriate behaviors.
3. It decreases the probability that the manager will resort to negative, coercive procedures in his or her efforts to manage.
4. It increases the likelihood that the manager will be successful in a situation where failure and chaos have been the norm in the past.

This does not mean that token systems are effective for all behaviors in all situations. But, as the author points out in his text, token systems are extremely effective in establishing improved behavior in difficult-to-manage situations.

In summary, we are delighted to include Dr. Ayllon's contribution to this series. **How to Set Up a Token Economy** will provide the reader with a clear road map for using this functional and effective behavioral procedure.

R. Vance Hall
January, 1982

How to Set Up a Token Economy

Why a Token Economy?

As caring individuals we strive to let those around us know when their behavior is appropriate. We truly want them to experience positive consequences for trying to reach a desired goal. However, in trying to meet the many demands placed upon us as parents, teachers and professionals, it frequently becomes difficult or impossible to provide an immediate "pay-off" for an individual's attempt to improve his or her behavior.

Parents want to show their son that they appreciate his assuming responsibility for household chores, but they feel they must wait and express their appreciation with an allowance at the first of the month. Teachers want to provide a special privilege for a child who has completed a difficult assignment after many weeks of work. Report cards are months away and they wish there were other ways to give their students daily recognition for their efforts. The psychiatric nurse notices that a patient has made several attempts to communicate with others. She wants to find a way to immediately encourage this behavior but does not know how to do so. She must wait to tell the doctor in her weekly report.

We frequently want to give others rewards for their personal improvement. We know it is important to do so immediately, however, daily demands often make this impossible. What is needed is a bridge between a desired behavior and a reward. There is a way to say "your behavior will be rewarded." This book provides information to assist you in giving such approval through a token system.

The techniques presented in this book are based on years of research conducted in real-life settings. This research has involved parents, teachers, and persons in institutional environments where token economies increased skills in children, students, and patients.

The exercises in this book can be used alone or under the direction of a professional who has a background in behavior management. If you master the techniques presented you should be able to more effectively provide immediate positive feedback to those around you and increase their functional living skills.

What is a Token Economy?

At Home

Alonzo was a black, fifteen-year-old male. He had been diagnosed as having **Conduct Disorder**, with aggressive features. He refused to attend classes and was extremely hostile toward school. He cursed and actively resisted being taken to school. He insisted that school was worth nothing. He wanted to get a job to earn money to buy a car. However, Alonzo did not have the skills or academic background to make him employable. He spent his days and nights watching television and fantasizing about a job and car. Scoldings from his mother and threats from school personnel brought no changes. The school psychologist suggested that Alonzo earn his allowance by attending school. He received a daily report from classes attended. His mother was to pay him daily for each class. For the first time Alonzo earned his allowance by just being in class. His attendance increased and he viewed school as his present job. His mother ceased nagging and was proud that her son was earning the money she once gave him. Alonzo was earning money for his car and acquiring skills that would enable him to function as an adult.

At School

Jimmy was a fifth-grade student in a suburban elementary school. He was qualified to attend a special class for the gifted, but could not adapt to the class even though his intelligence tests and achievement tests indicated he was very bright and capable. His teachers complained about his daydreaming and his inability to complete daily assignments. His grades were poor and his teachers considered him to be lazy and unmotivated. He spent his time drawing pictures of space heroes and building imaginary space capsules. His teachers decided to give Jimmy a point for each classroom assignment completed with ninety percent accuracy. The points were to be exchanged after lunch each day. Each point was worth ten minutes to work on a project for science. Jimmy worked to get access to the science project and to share his creations with the rest of the class during the science period. Jimmy's teachers were pleased that he had learned to complete his work and make good grades. He took pride in sharing his projects with the class. His improvement allowed him to begin attending the special class for the gifted.

In An Institution

Mary was a sixty-year-old, chronic schizophrenic patient in a midwestern hospital. She had spent twenty-five years there and had received various treatments, including electro-shock therapy and drug therapy, without success. She spent most of her time in an unkempt state doing nothing but sitting on the side of her bed. Efforts to interest her in self-care, work and recreation activities had failed. Lack of interest in self and lack of motivation to interact with others is characteristic of schizophrenic patients. Mary's behavior was typical of those with her diagnosis. When a program was established on her ward to pay tokens for getting dressed and communicating with others she began to do so. She gradually learned personal grooming and began to work as a kitchen assistant. In her job she interacted with the kitchen staff. Mary exchanged her tokens for new clothes and for furnishings for her room. She liked being paid for her performance and learned skills that she would be able to use outside the hospital.

These three incidents illustrate the use of token economies to increase appropriate behavior, in the home, in school and in an institution.

Can you think of incidents from your own experience that illustrate the use of token economies? _____

_____

_____

_____

_____

_____

_____

_____

_____

_____

_____

_____

_____

_____

Defining the Token Economy

A token economy is a motivational system that uses tokens to bridge the delay between a desired behavior and a reward for that behavior. Tokens immediately follow the appropriate response and are later exchanged for activities, privileges or commodities that are rewarding to the individual. Tokens may be plastic chips, stars, stamps, points, check marks, happy faces, play money, and other distinct units. These items function as rewards by being associated with a "pay-off." Tokens function as money does in our society. An individual receives a token for a desirable behavior. He learns immediately that there is an incentive to repeat the behavior that earned the token. At a later time tokens are exchanged for self-selected rewards.

List below any items you can think of that could be used in a token economy. _____

_____

_____

_____

_____

_____

_____

_____

_____

_____

_____

_____

_____

_____

_____

_____

_____

_____

Exercise 1: Define a Token Economy

What is a token economy? _____

_____

_____

_____

_____

_____

_____

_____

_____

You are on the right track if you said a token economy is a system of exchange where an individual's positive behavior results in credits which can later be cashed in for a variety of rewards.

List some items that might serve as tokens in your setting.

_____

_____

_____

_____

_____

_____

_____

_____

_____

If you are in a school setting you might have selected points, stars, check marks or a special ink stamp. In the home you could have used trading stamps, plastic chips from a game or bottle caps. Institutions would possibly select plastic coins that could be easily carried and yet difficult to duplicate.

Now that you know how a token economy influences the behavior of others, you are ready to learn the basic steps to increase a specific behavior in someone you know.

Basic Steps in
Establishing a Token Economy

STEP ONE: IDENTIFY TARGET BEHAVIORS
(What Do I Want To See Happen)

It is necessary to focus on one or more positive behaviors that you want to increase. Ask yourself what do you want the person to be doing. Select behaviors that have value in the real world. In defining these behaviors, be specific. Focus on a behavior you can observe and count. Avoid the use of vague labels such as "uncooperative," "defiant," "unmotivated." Pinpoint a positive behavior you want to increase. Think Positively!

Instead of saying you would "like Sarah to stop being so lazy," indicate constructive behaviors you want Sarah to exhibit. When identifying behaviors, tell who, what, where, when (Hall & Hall, 1980).

Mr. and Mrs. Thomas were concerned about their three-year-old son Bobby. He would not stay in bed at night. As soon as they placed him in his bed and left the room he followed them out into the family room. This continued for many weeks and resulted in a loss of sleep for the entire family. Spanking and reprimands did not work. Bobby continued to get out of bed night after night.

Mrs. Jones was asked to define a target behavior. She stated that she wanted Bobby to stop wandering around the house at night. When asked specifically what she wanted to see Bobby do differently she suggested remaining in his bed when taken there at 8 p.m. Mrs. Jones then focused on a positive behavior she wanted to increase. Her definition told who, what, where, and when. Bobby was the **who.** Remaining in bed was the **what.** In his room was the **where.** The **when** was 8 p.m.

Why is it important to be precise and positive in identifying target behaviors? _____

_____

_____

_____

_____

_____

Exercise 2: Identifying Target Behaviors to Increase Their Frequency

In the following examples identify a target behavior that will earn tokens when a token economy is in effect.

At Home

Mrs. Turner was distressed because her fifteen-year-old daughter left her clothes and personal belongings scattered about her room. Clothes were never in drawers or closets, but were thrown about the room. Nothing was in its proper place. Her furniture and floors could not be cleaned until things were picked up. Mrs. Turner gave up reminding her daughter and threatening to take away privileges, however, she was tired of doing all the work herself. She was also angry because her daughter was not assuming responsibility for taking care of her possessions. She knew something had to change.

What target behavior could Mrs. Turner identify?

Who?_____

What? _____

_____

_____

Where? _____

When?_____

Did you identify a specific behavior such as putting personal possessions in their designated places?_____Yes _____No You might have said Mrs. Turner's daughter will put her clothes and belongings in their proper places every afternoon when she returns from school. Remember to focus on a specific positive behavior that will enable you to see a change. Mrs. Turner needs to be able to look in her daughter's room and observe the results of new behaviors.

At School

Mr. Roberts enjoyed teaching his fifth period science class at the middle school. He had excellent students and their grades were superior. He felt the class could accomplish even more if everyone arrived on time. Ten to fifteen minutes of instruction

time was lost daily because students wandered in late. He was
tired of waiting for them to get settled so his lecture could begin.

What target behavior could Mr. Roberts pinpoint?

Who?_____

What? _____

_____

Where? _____

_____

When?_____

Did you identify a specific behavior such as arriving in class on time? If so, good for you!

In an Institution

Thelma refused to talk to other patients on her ward or communicate her needs to the hospital staff. She spent her days sitting in the activity room watching television. When others approached her she ignored their presence. Thelma would not participate in individual or group therapy sessions. When she had entered the hospital seven years ago she talked to others, but she gradually became nonverbal. The staff was quite concerned and believed her return to a more normal setting was not likely to occur unless she learned to communicate again.

As a staff member of the hospital, what is one target behavior you would like Thelma to increase?

Who?_____

What? _____

_____

Where? _____

_____

When?_____

One behavior could be to have Thelma talk to others.

Examples of Target Behaviors

At Home

Complete homework before playing.
Feed animals.
Take out the trash.
Put toys in toy chest when finished playing.
Clear the table.
Read one hour each night.
Be in bed at designated time.
Follow instructions without talking back.
Put soiled clothes in laundry hamper.
Wash the dishes.
Clear the table after meals.
Brush teeth and bathe without assistance.
Remain at the table until everyone is finished.
Get up and dressed after being called once.
Make bed each morning.
Mow the lawn once a week.
Ask permission to use the car.

At School

Complete assignments daily.
Be in class on time.
Come to class with materials.
Raise hand to be recognized.
Keep area around desk clean.
Obey class rules.

In an Institution

Dress self.
Make bed.
Bathe self.
Talk to other patients.
Participate in group therapy.
Go to the dining room unassisted.
Feed self.
Write letters.
Participate in exercise class.
Complete assigned job.

Now it is your turn to identify a target behavior you would like to change in a setting that is important to you.

Who?_____

What? _____

_____

_____

_____

_____

_____

_____

_____

Where? _____

_____

_____

_____

_____

_____

When?_____

_____

_____

Have someone working with you check your work. If you had difficulty, perhaps you selected a situation that was too complex. Begin with a behavior that is easy to identify. Can you define the positive behavior you want to increase? If so, put a check here ☐. If not, you should review the previous section.

STEP TWO: DEFINE TOKENS

You have now determined which behaviors you want to strengthen. It is time to select an appropriate medium of exchange for your particular setting. Tokens are like money. They are exchanged for an item or activity that is rewarding to the individual. There are guidelines that must be followed in the selection of appropriate tokens.

Rule 1: Tokens must be easily available. Tokens must be objects or symbols readily available. Tokens include such things as poker chips, plastic coins from a board game, credits in a credit card system, points or checkmarks on a tally sheet, special stamps, even play money. It is essential that the individual be able to see and count the value of the tokens.

Rule 2: Tokens must be easy to administer. It is essential for the person delivering tokens to have them handy at all times. One of the principal components of a token economy is that appropriate behavior is reinforced **immediately!** The person dispensing the reinforcement does not have time to search for tokens. They must be available constantly because tokens are used primarily to bridge the gap between the time a desired behavior occurs and the reinforcement which follows. The teacher can have a magic marker in his or her pocket to place checks on a tally sheet. A mother can carry plastic game chips in her apron. The ward attendant can have imitation coins to give patients wherever they may be. Tokens should not be cumbersome or expensive. They can be as simple as colored sheets of paper cut in special shapes.

Rule 3: Tokens must be difficult to duplicate by those receiving them. Tokens, like money, lose their value if they can easily be counterfeited. One must select tokens unique in a particular setting. If you choose to use check marks or stars, you should select colors that are not available to students, children or patients. Change colors daily. You might want to use your initials on a tally sheet. Your handwriting would be difficult to duplicate.

Rule 4: Tokens need to be nontransferrable. Tokens must be of value only in your exchange system.

Rule 5: Keep a record of the tokens earned and spent. This will provide you with the information you need to increase or decrease the amount of reinforcement to be most effective.

What can you use to bridge the gap between the desired behavior when it takes place and the reinforcement for it? _____

_____

_____

_____

_____

_____

A student told his teacher that he would feel more motivated to do his school work if he received his tokens before completing his assignment. What would you suggest the teacher do? _____

_____

_____

_____

_____

The staff of a psychiatric ward had a problem with a patient who did not earn tokens but stole them from other patients. What would you do? _____

_____

_____

_____

_____

_____

If you are not sure about your answers, please reread the last section.

Now that you have some basic rules for selecting tokens (currency), try to apply the five rules in the following exercise.

Exercise 3: Selection of Tokens

List items or symbols that could serve as tokens in your particular setting. Remember the five basic rules:

_____

_____

_____

_____

I selected these tokens because:

_____

_____

_____

_____

_____

_____

_____

_____

_____

_____

_____

_____

_____

_____

_____

If you remembered the five rules you probably have an effective token. To check yourself answer the following questions.

1. My token was easily available. Yes_____ No_____

2. My token was easy to administer. Yes_____ No_____

3. My token was difficult to duplicate. Yes_____ No_____

4. My token was nontransferrable. Yes_____ No_____

5. My token was easy to keep records on. Yes_____ No_____

STEP THREE: IDENTIFYING ITEMS, PRIVILEGES AND OTHER INCENTIVES FOR REWARDING APPROPRIATE BEHAVIORS

Now that you have identified specific behaviors to change, it is necessary to determine the pay-off for the tokens. This is an especially critical step. When students, children, and patients receive their tokens they must be exchanged for items or privileges that are rewarding. How do you determine which activities or items will increase the behaviors we desire to increase?

One effective method for determining what may be motivating to an individual is to observe what the individual chooses to do throughout the day when under no particular demands. There is a high probability that those activities are chosen by an individual as a reward. The history teacher will tell you that his junior high students use any free time to chat together about ball games, movies, and the next big dance. He often rewards his class for working well by letting them have ten minutes of free time at the end of the period. At home a father notices that his twins spend their afternoons watching a particular television show or playing ball with the children next door. On the ward, the day nurse notices Mrs. Jones spending hours reading movie magazines. Simply observing the activities of persons will give you a good indication of privileges to plan as rewards for them.

Have you noticed persons you live or work with engaging in activities that you might use as rewards for them? If so, what are

they? _____

_____

_____

_____

_____

_____

Another procedure involves asking the individual to tell what is personally rewarding. You may want to establish a routine to give children or residents an opportunity to express their needs. There are numerous ways of providing these opportunities. One might select a definite time each week to interview the individual and let him verbally express preferences. An equally effective and less time-consuming procedure is to use a reward questionnaire such as the following.

Reward Questionnaire

Name _____ Date _____

If I could choose an activity or privilege, I would like to do the following:

_____

_____

_____

_____

If I could choose an item that I would like to have for my own I would want (You may include books, magazines, food, toys, games)

_____

_____

_____

_____

_____

_____

_____

_____

_____

You must remember that an event or object may appear to be rewarding to you, but may not be rewarding to someone else. There is a distinct difference between a reward and a reinforcer. A reward may be something you subjectively believe to be pleasing to an individual. A reinforcer is an event or item that leads to an **increase** in a desired behavior. It is essential that our rewards bring about an increase in target behavior and therefore become reinforcers. Guidelines for selecting rewards tell us to **look** and **listen.** Here are a few exercises to assist you in determining what are effective rewards.

Exercise 4: Selecting Rewards

At Home

Mrs. Taylor had pinpointed a target behavior for her six-year-old son, John. She wanted him to complete his meals. She considered him to be a picky eater. He would eat a little of the foods he liked and then ask for dessert. The rest of the children finished the main course and then received a dessert of fruit, yogurt or a milk pudding. John hurried through his meal and was the first to ask for dessert.

By watching John's behavior at meals Mrs. Taylor hoped to find a reward for the target behavior of John completing the main course. What would you choose as a reward for John?

_____

_____

If you selected dessert as a reward for John you are right.

At School

Sally was an extremely shy twelve year old. She talked in class only when called on. In the cafeteria she usually sat at a table by herself. When at a table with others she was left out of the conversation. Mrs. Harris, the teacher, wanted Sally to socialize at lunch. She wanted to see Sally talking to others. She asked Sally one afternoon if there was anyone she would feel comfortable talking to at lunch. Sally replied that Mary, the most popular girl in the class, was her neighborhood friend. Sally could never sit by Mary because the other children hurried to Mary's table.

If you were Sally's teacher what privilege might you use to increase Sally's social interaction?

_____

_____

_____

_____

_____

_____

_____

_____

_____

_____

_____

You might have let Sally choose a friend to sit with at lunch. Sally could have the opportunity to tell you daily with whom she would like to sit. She may initially choose Mary and perhaps once she begins to interact she may feel comfortable with others. As is true in many cases, Mrs. Harris had to ask Sally what would be meaningful to her in order to find an effective reinforcer.

In an Institution

When the ward attendant asked Agnes (a retarded adult) what she would like, Agnes replied there was nothing she wanted. Agnes said that she had everything she needed. The attendant decided to watch Agnes throughout the day. The attendant observed Agnes stealing cigarettes from the other patients whenever the opportunity arose.

What could the attendant select as a reward for Agnes?

_____

_____

_____

_____

_____

_____

_____

_____

Even though Agnes was unable to communicate her needs, the nurse observed that cigarettes were important to her.

Exercise 5: Finding Rewards You Can Use

- Observe someone in your setting throughout the day. Watch what they do in their free time and observe activities and items they choose.
- Ask the individual what privileges he or she likes and what items he or she would select to use for a time or to own.
- From your observation and your interview, designate one or more rewards for this individual.

From my observation I think the following activities and items should be appropriate rewards _____

_____

_____

_____

_____

_____

_____

_____

From my interview it appears that the following activities and items would be appropriate rewards _____

_____

_____

_____

_____

_____

_____

Are your lists the same? Perhaps not. The true test for determining what is rewarding is to experiment with a wide range of choices and allow the individual to select his or her own pay-off. You will learn how to do this in the following section.

Examples of Rewards at Home

Television time (in minutes).
Staying up late.
Free time.
Request for favorite dish.
Dessert.
A meal at a favorite restaurant.
Movie.
Skating.
Records.
Time **alone** with parent.

Attend a sports event.
Choice of clothes to wear.
Choice of clothes to buy.
Guest overnight.
Spending night at home of a
  friend.
Having a friend over for a meal.
New toy.
Car privileges.
Bike privileges.

At School

Writing on chalkboard.
Finger painting.
Using typewriter.
Watching a movie.
Tutoring a younger child.
Eating with a friend.
Extra free time.
Sitting with the teacher
  at lunch.
Helping the librarian, secretary
  or custodian.
Listening to records with
  headphones.

Playing a special game.
Being teacher for a lesson.
Cleaning the erasers.
Watering plants.
Operating slide projector.
Being excused from a test.
Watching television.
Having a popcorn party.
Getting a "good note" to take
  home.
Being leader of a game.
Going to the library.
Collecting and grading papers.

In an Institution

Choice of special foods.
Opportunity for privacy.
Commissary item such as
  cigarettes, candy, soft
  drinks and magazines.
Television time.
Choice of company
  at meals.
Special clothes.
A locked cabinet.

Extra time with psychologist or
  other staff member.
Phone calls.
Ground privileges.
A special chair.
Attending chapel.
Playing cards.
Selecting a job.
Visiting the barber or beauty
  shop.

Exercise 6: Identifying Rewards to Use in Your Token Economy

List all the activities, items and privileges you might use in your token economy. Think of all the individuals in your setting and consider what you **see** them doing and **hear** them requesting. Name as many rewards as you can.

You saw them doing: _____

_____

_____

_____

_____

_____

_____

You heard them request: _____

_____

_____

_____

_____

_____

_____

Other items and privileges you have identified: _____

_____

_____

_____

_____

_____

_____

_____

STEP FOUR: PLANNING AN EXCHANGE SYSTEM

At this point you know how to pinpoint a target behavior, select reinforcing items and activities, and provide a bridge between the two by giving immediate pay-off in the form of a token. Now it is essential to learn how to put these components together. The result will be a token economy. To put your system together ask yourself the following questions:

1. Have I defined target behaviors for the individuals involved? Yes_____ No_____
2. Have I described these behaviors specifically so I can observe a change? Yes_____ No_____
3. Have I concentrated on positive behaviors I would like to have increased and avoided negative behaviors? Yes_____ No_____
4. Have I determined activities and privileges that would be reinforcing (rewarding) to the individuals involved? Yes_____ No_____
5. Have I designated tokens (currency) that can be readily available when the individual performs the desired behavior? Yes_____ No_____
6. Are these tokens easily available? Yes_____ No_____
7. Are they easy to administer? Yes_____ No_____
8. Are these tokens difficult to duplicate? Yes_____ No_____
9. Are they nontransferrable? Yes_____ No_____
10. Are they easy to keep track of? Yes_____ No_____

If you answered **yes** to all of the questions you are ready for this step. If you answered **no** to any question, read the section again and perhaps obtain assistance from your instructor or a fellow worker in your setting.

You must plan an exchange system for the tokens by doing the following:

1. Specify what performance is required to receive a token or tokens.

2. Make sure that tokens will **immediately** follow the desired response. This is essential!

3. Place a value on all privileges and commodities. Individuals must know how many tokens they must earn to get their reward.

4. Specify a time and place for the exchange to occur and who will monitor the exchange.

What four things must you do when planning your exchange system?

1. _____

_____

2. _____

_____

3. _____

_____

4. _____

_____

You may have difficulty placing a value on activities and items. The ability to do this comes with practice and through trial and error. One way to determine how much behavior you should require for the pay-off is to offer students, children and patients several items with varying costs. You might want to construct a menu of items and privileges to be purchased with the acquired tokens. Use a wide range of alternatives and use many variations of a particular reward. If you know Tommy likes candy, have a selection that includes many different kinds of candy. Try to change the reinforcement menu regularly. When an individual has too much of an item he becomes satiated and bored with it and the item loses its value. You may like spaghetti, but if you eat only spaghetti day after day it loses its appeal. The key is to **use many variations** of the reinforcer. The following examples will assist you in placing values on your rewards and creating your own reinforcement menu.

At Home

Mr. Rudder established a token economy for his nine-year-old son, Tim, who had neglected to assume responsibility for his household chores. He and his father decided that each task completed would be worth points that could be cashed in for privileges. On the refrigerator door Mr. Rudder placed the following description of desired behaviors, their value, and what they could purchase daily. Tim marked off his tasks as he completed them and then told Mr. Rudder how he would like to exchange his points. Mr. Rudder checked the list and the completion of tasks when he arrived home each evening.

```
┌─────────────────────────────────────────────────────────────┐
│                        Tim's List                            │
│                                                              │
│       My daily jobs                            Points        │
│    1. Make my bed.                               1           │
│    2. Put games on shelf.                        2           │
│    3. Take out trash.                            1           │
│    4. Clear the table at dinner.                 2           │
│    5. Feed the animals.                          2           │
│    ---------------------------------------------------       │
│       The points I earned may be exchanged for the following:│
│       Selecting my favorite television show for all to       │
│       watch                                      3           │
│       Staying up one hour past my bedtime to read in         │
│       my room.                                   3           │
│       Riding my bike to the store.               3           │
│       Selecting my favorite dish.                2           │
│       Having a friend to spend the night.        25          │
│       Going to my favorite fast-food restaurant. 40          │
│       Buying a new baseball glove.               120         │
│       Spending the night in the guest room.      11          │
│                                                              │
│    Dad and I agree on my list of jobs and my rewards:        │
│       Signed _____    _____            │
└─────────────────────────────────────────────────────────────┘
```

Tim could cash his points in each day for rewards or save them for larger rewards. Many children and adults are rewarded by watching their points grow. Tim might choose to cash in three points each night for watching his favorite show, and save the remaining points for a later treat, such as having a friend spend the night. Tim and his father together decided upon privileges that would be meaningful and realistic. Once Tim began earning points he decided to save his points over a period of time for a larger reward, a camp-out with his father. They decided such a trip was worth 160 points. This meant that Tim had approximately four weeks of completing all his tasks. Even though the camping trip was weeks away, Tim was pleased with his **immediate** pay-off, earning points daily. Mr. Rudder was pleased to see Tim assuming responsibility and was glad that he no longer had to scold or threaten to take away privileges. Tim was delighted to have the opportunity to earn fun things. He no longer viewed household responsibilities as a burden. He knew he was doing his share!

At School

This was the year that Mrs. Reams had the "immature" class. Her pupils were in their third year of school, but behaved as if they were first-grade students. No one completed the assignments. Mrs. Reams spent most of her time breaking up fights, reminding students to be quiet, and pleading with them to finish their work. The school counselor suggested that Mrs. Reams establish a token economy to increase the number of assignments completed. She said that if students were rewarded for doing their work they would perhaps spend less time fighting and talking. Mrs. Reams liked the idea. She and the counselor made the chart shown on page 25 and posted it on the wall for everyone to see.

At 2:00 each day Mrs. Reams checked the students' folders. This took approximately 15 minutes. Students had to earn at least two points to participate. Those with less than two points remained at their desks completing work. Students received a ticket with the number of points earned written on it. They wrote their choice of activity below the number and gave it to a monitor who checked to see that they were requesting an activity they had earned. The reinforcement period was the last thirty minutes of the day, a time when students usually finished work and gathered their belongings to prepare for bus call. Mrs. Reams changed the menu weekly, sometimes adjusting the point values of the activities as she learned which activities were the most rewarding. The students worked hard to earn their activities at the end of the day. As a result the entire atmosphere in the class changed. Mrs. Reams spent most of her time instructing students and little time with discipline. She could not believe how her class had changed!

The students helped her operate the token economy. They became competitive about earning points. They also monitored each other's behavior. On Friday afternoons the students helped Mrs. Reams plan the activities for next week's menu.

Mrs. Ream's token economy was at no expense to her. She watched to see what activities students enjoyed, asked them to express their priorities, and required that they earn the time to participate.

In an Institution

Mrs. Taylor, R.N., established a token economy for Lena, a 50-year old schizophrenic patient hospitalized for 20 years. The

Point System

At 2:00 I shall check each student's work folder and award points for all assignments completed. There are normally eight assignments each day. Students will have the privilege of earning points that will be traded at 2:15.

Task	Point Value
Assignment completed	1
Assignment completed with 80% accuracy or more.	2

Points will buy the following at 2:15

Menu

Dust erasers.	2
Clean chalk board.	2
Water flowers.	2
Use water colors at desk.	2
Empty trash.	3
Sweep the floor.	3
Play with the clay.	4
Serve as teacher aide.	4
Go to the library.	4
Listen to records with headphones.	4
Play with puppets.	4
Watch television.	5
Carry messages.	5
Do a science experiment.	5
Feed animals in the room.	6
Clean teacher's desk.	6
Take the flag down.	7
Read stories to younger children.	7
Play an electronic game.	8
Select any toy at the free-time center.	8
Assist the secretary.	8
Assist the custodian.	8
Give the end of the day report on the intercom.	8
Assist the teacher in monitoring the activities.	8
A good note home plus free time.	8

nurse and her staff wanted Lena to be responsible for her appearance and to learn job-related skills. Therefore, the staff decided on a list of goals and a reinforcement menu.

Lena's Goals

Self Care

Combs hair. Wears dress, slip, panties, bra, stockings and shoes (inspection at meal time). 1 token per time

Bathing. Takes bath at time designated for bath. 1 token

Tooth brushing. Brushes teeth or gargles at time designated for it, once daily. 1 token

Exercises. Participates in exercises conducted by the exercise assistant (twice daily). 1 token

Bed making. Makes own bed and cleans area around and under bed. 1 token

Job-Related Skills

Beauty aide. Assists in shampooing, setting and combing hair for patients who desire special service. 4 tokens

Physical exercises. Operates record player and leads patients in group exercises at designated times and place. 10 tokens

Clothing assistant. Sets up ironing board and iron. Irons clothing that belongs to other patients. Folds clothing neatly. Returns ironed clothing, iron and ironing board to nurses's station. 6 tokens

Reinforcement Menu

Selection of room 1 (least desirable)	No tokens
Selection of room 2	4 tokens daily
Selection of room 3	8 tokens daily
Selection of room 4	15 tokens daily
Selection of room 5 (most desirable)	30 tokens daily
Room divider	1 token
Selection of chair	1 token
Choice of bedspread	1 token
Walk on hospital grounds (15 mins.)	2 tokens
Consumable items such as candy, cigarettes, juice, iced-tea, coffee.	1-5 tokens

Each two weeks, a staff member met with Lena to review her progress and to give her a choice of new job-related assignments adjusted to her skill repertoire and motivational level.

Exercise 7: Preparing a Reinforcement Menu

- Think of items and activities that you could give in exchange for tokens.
- List all of the possibilities.
- Assign a value to each.
- Decide upon a time and place for your token exchange.
- Determine who will monitor this exchange.

Tokens may be traded   Value
for the following:

_____

_____

_____

_____

_____

_____

_____

_____

_____

_____

Tokens will be exchanged at the following time(s): _____

_____

_____

The place for exchange is_____

_____

_____

The individual who will monitor the exchange is _____

_____

_____

_____

_____

Points to Remember

Adjust your requirements so that it is possible for everyone to earn a token. You may have to begin with a small portion of the desired behavior. You can gradually increase the amount of behavior necessary to earn a token.

At Home

Mrs. Jones wanted Samantha to pick up her toys that were scattered all over the house and yard. Mrs. Jones knew that she must not require too much at first or Samantha would give up. Instead of having Samantha earn points for picking up all of her toys, she began by concentrating on toys outside. After Samantha began earning points for this target behavior, Mrs. Jones added an additional requirement of Samantha picking up toys in her room.

At School

Coach Preston wanted David to play by the rules in physical education. He knew that David was easily frustrated and could not go for very long without recognition. He decided to focus on one rule for David to achieve in his class. He knew that David was good at following directions, so he gave David a point each time he followed a verbal request. If David earned a designated number of points he could assist the coach in putting the equipment away. When David mastered that goal the coach added an additional rule.

In an Institution

The ward attendant was concerned that Douglas would not communicate with any of the staff. The attendant's goal was to have Douglas verbally express his needs. Realizing this long-range goal was immediately unachievable, he decided to administer tokens for eye contact. Every time Douglas looked at the person speaking to him, he received a token and verbal praise. The first few times the attendant had to gently move Douglas' head so that he was looking at him. Once Douglas began earning tokens for looking at the person talking to him, he was required to nod and later still, a "yes" or "no" to questions was expected.

Administer tokens immediately after the desired response.

At Home

Mrs. Johnson wanted Jenny, her two-year old to go to the toilet by herself. Whenever Mrs. Johnson observed Jenny doing this she gave her a plastic chip with which Jenny could later purchase fun activities.

At School

Mr. James wanted Cynthia to clean up around her desk. Cynthia made good grades but could not keep her school supplies in the proper place. Whenever Mr. James saw Cynthia picking up books, paper and other supplies he gave her a check mark on her tally sheet. She traded these at the end of the day for a special game.

In an Institution

Mildred liked to start arguments with the other patients. The nurse wanted Mildred to converse with the others in a positive manner. Whenever she observed Mildred talking with other patients she gave her a token to be traded in for cigarettes or magazines.

Activities and commodities used as reinforcers must be made available only through tokens. They should not be free.

At Home

Mrs. Anderson could not understand why Alice had stopped earning points for a special afternoon snack. After talking with the mother of Alice's friend down the street, she realized what had happened. Alice was stopping by her friend's house on the way home from school. There she enjoyed a snack that was free!

At School

The math teacher at a middle school attempted to establish a token economy. Something was wrong! Students received points for work completed. These points could be exchanged for candy. But few students earned the required points. The math teacher knew the students liked candy, for he found candy wrappers on the floor and in the trash can. Then he realized that the students did not have to earn candy. They brought it to school in their pockets!

In an Institution

John, an 18-year-old in an adolescent unit, was on a token system, but according to the staff, he was not motivated to earn the tokens. His parents sent him money which he spent on the same items that the tokens could be exchanged for. The way the staff solved the problem was to open a bank account for John and set a limit on bank withdrawals. Each week he could withdraw $5.00 in exchange for a specific number of tokens. This meant that John still needed to earn tokens in order to gain access to his bank account.

Points to Consider if Problems Occur

Problems may arise in establishing a token economy. However, if you know how to handle them in advance, they are easily overcome.

1. Did you provide tokens during or immediately following the desired behavior? Yes_____ No_____

Remember that tokens enable you to provide reinforcement **immediately.** In order to obtain an increase in behavior, frequent reinforcement is necessary until the desired level is reached.

2. How are you maintaining your token economy?

Two points must be considered. First, it is essential to adjust the reinforcement menu periodically. Items and privileges should be varied to prevent satiation or boredom. Second, the number of tokens required to earn these items may need to be altered from time to time. For example, an individual may earn tokens at one point and then quit. This situation may be caused by too low a value on the reinforcers (they are too easy to earn). By increasing the cost of popular items, more tokens will be required to earn them. You may also find an individual's behavior improving when he is not earning sufficient tokens to purchase desired items. In order to maintain this improvement, you will need to increase the token value of target behaviors or decrease the cost of items on the menu.

3. What do you do if an individual indicates he will not participate in the token system?

This is less likely to occur if the persons earning the tokens have some responsibility in setting up the token economy. Participants may assist in selecting the reinforcers available for the token exchange. Research indicates that those who initially protest will participate once they begin earning rewards or observe others doing so. The best strategy is to proceed with the system and ignore the verbal behavior of those who protest. Their behavior will most likely change when they see that the only way to obtain highly desired privileges and activities is by earning tokens.

4. What if your token system is too costly in terms of time and effort to administer it?

In most instances, the simpler the token system, the more success-ful it is likely to be. When possible, plan a system that enables individual participants to assist with the management. Some token economies can be run entirely by the students. Ayllon and Azrin (1968) had patients operate the concession stand. Individuals can use tokens to purchase privileges that are a part of the system. They can dispense tokens, set up reinforcement activities and monitor the exchange of tokens for reinforcers.

5. **How do you gain the interest and participation of persons who are deprived or severely handicapped?**

It may be necessary to use token reinforcement samplings to get your token economy going when an individual has had limited contact with the available reinforcers. Ayllon and Azrin (1968) let patients who would not pay tokens to watch a movie sample a free movie. Movies then became a favorite item on the reinforcement menu. With severely handicapped persons, it may be necessary to physically prompt the desired behavior, present the token selected, and immediately carry out the exchange. Once this chain has been established, the time between earning the token and the exchange for the reinforcer can gradually be lengthened.

6. **How do you fade out the token system?**

Token systems should be modified or faded out once the desired behaviors have become a regular part of the person's repertoire and are being maintained by more natural consequences for good performance. For example, one parent who had established a token system with her three young children reported she was still using the system four years later although the behaviors and reinforcers had changed dramatically and the system was almost entirely self-administered by the children (Hall, 1971).

One way of fading the token system is to gradually delay the opportunity for exchange. Phillips et al. (1968), in their Teaching Family Program for pre-delinquent adolescents, faded residents from the token system by shifting from a daily earning of privileges to a weekly earning of privileges to an honor system in which no token exchange was used if appropriate behavior was maintained at an acceptable level.

Pairing social reinforcers with the delivery of tokens is also important if behaviors are to be maintained in natural settings. Delivery of the token should be accompanied by a statement praising a specific behavior, e.g., "Here is a token for your good work," or a smile, a pat on the back, or other social reinforcer.

Selecting items and privileges that are likely to occur in a variety of settings also makes it easier to shift from a token system. The reinforcement menu may initially have trinkets and tangible items that have fixed prices. When more activities and privileges are included in the menu, these are likely to occur as a natural pay-off in a number of settings. For more information on selecting reinforcers, see **How to Select Reinforcers,** by Hall and Hall (1980).

Review

Plan your own token economy by following these steps:

1. Identify target behavior(s).

_____

_____

_____

_____

2. Designate back-up reinforcers (activities, items, food).

_____

_____

_____

3. Describe your medium of exchange. What will you use as tokens?

_____

_____

_____

4. Establish a value for your reinforcers. How much behavior will be required for each?

_____

_____

_____

5. Who will administer the tokens?

_____

_____

6. When and where will the exchange(s) of tokens for reinforcers take place?

_____

_____

7. Who will monitor the exchange?

_____

_____

_____

References

Ayllon, T. and Azrin, N. The measurement and reinforcement of behavior of psychotics. **Journal of Experimental Analysis of Behavior,** 1965, **8,** 357-383.

Ayllon, T. and Azrin, N. **The Token Economy: A Motivational System for Therapy and Rehabilitation,** Appleton-Century-Crofts, New York, 1968.

Ayllon, T. and Azrin, N. Reinforcer sampling: a technique for increasing the behavior of mental patients. **Journal of Applied Behavior Analysis,** 1968, **1,** 13-20.

Ayllon, T., Smith, D., and Rogers, W. Behavior management of school phobia. **Journal of Behavior Therapy and Experimental Psychiatry,** 1970, **1,** 125-138.

Ayllon, T., Layman, D., and Burke, S. Disruptive behavior and reinforcement of academic performance. **The Psychological Record,** 1972, **22,** 315-323.

Ayllon, T. and Roberts, M. D. Eliminating discipline problems by strengthening academic performance. **The Journal of Applied Behavior Analysis,** 1974, **7,** 71-76.

Ayllon, T., Layman, D., and Kandel, H. A behavioral educational alternative to drug control of hyperactive children. **The Journal of Applied Behavior Analysis,** 1975, **8,** 137-146.

Ayllon, T., Garber, S. and Pisor, K. The elimination of discipline problems through a combined school-home motivational system. **Behavior Therapy,** 1975, **6,** 616-626.

Ayllon, T. and Garber, S. Teaching reading through a student-administered point system, in **New Developments in Behavioral Research,** in B. C. Etzel, J. M. LeBlanc, and D. M. Baer (Eds.), Hillsdale, New Jersey: Lawrence Erlbaum Associates, 1977.

Ayllon, T., Garber, S. and Allison, M. Behavioral treatment of childhood neurosis. **Psychiatry,** 1977, **40,** 315-322.

Ayllon, T. and Rosenbaum, M. The behavioral treatment of disruption and hyperactivity in school settings, in **Advances in Child Clinical Psychology,** in B. Lahey and A. Kazdin (Eds.), Plenum Publishing Co., N.Y., 1977.

Bushell, D., Wrobel, P. A. and Michaelis, M. L. Applying group contingencies to the classroom study of behavior of preschool children. **Journal of Applied Behavior Analysis,** 1968, **1,** 55-61.

Phillips, E. L. Achievement Place: token reinforcement procedures in a home-style rehabilitation setting for predelinquent boys. **Journal of Applied Behavior Analysis,** 1968, **1,** 213-223.

Wolfe, M. M., Giles, D. K. and Hall, R. V. Experiments with token reinforcement in a remedial classroom. **Behavior Research and Therapy,** 1968, **6,** 51-64.